GROOKS IV

PIET HEIN

GROOKS IV

With the assistance of Jens Arup

BORGEN'S BILLIGBØGER 117

The collections of
GROOKS
are published by
General Publishing Co. Ltd.
Ontario, Canada
Doubleday & Company, Inc.
New York, U.S.A.
Blackwell & Mott Ltd.
Oxford, England
and
BORGENS FORLAG
Copenhagen, Denmark

The grooks have now been printed in 290.000 copies

ISBN 87 418 1239 5 (hft.)
ISBN 87 418 1507 6 (indb.)

Rounborgs grafiske hus . Holstebro

PIET HEIN

40 books among which are
GRUK, ESPERANTO ELDONO
GRUK FRA ALLE ÅRENE 1
300 gruk, 1940—1964
GRUK FRA ALLE ÅRENE 2
300 gruk til, 1940—1964
GROOKS I
GROOKS II
GROOKS III
I FOLKEMUNDE, korte gruk I
DET KRAFTENS ORD, korte gruk II
RUNAWAY RUNES. Short grooks 1
GROOKS IN MUSIC
DIGTE FRA ALLE ÅRENE

THE GREAT AND THE SMALL

Grook in proportions

When great things
whose greatness
is destined to fall
have turned out
too little
to matter at all,
then stoop
and discover
the great in the small.

THE RECALCITRANT MEDIUM

The unyielding medium's
        not merely endured:
it's that upon which
        art depends.
For who can perform
        on a tightrope secured
only at one
        of its ends?

POPULAR RENOWN

Strive after popular renown,
        and you'll
have no attention left
        for things worth doing.
To have the fools
        consider you no fool
is a distinction
        hardly worth pursuing.

ROAD HOGS

Traffic grook

Does no one read the Highway Code?
Most people drive, without a care,
right in the middle of the road—
though they can see I'm driving there.

DATES

A box of dates
     embodies a
          malicious sense of fun.
You eat enough,
     you eat some more,
          you eat until you're done.
And then you go
     and wash your hands—
          and take another one.

THE COMMON WELL

To Charles Chaplin

The well you invite us to drink of
is one that no drop may be bought of.
You think of what all of us think of
but nobody else could have thought of.

UP TO THE MINUTE

We think of our age
as the age of all ages
when Man has grown modern at last.
But what other page
among History's pages
was so overburdened with past?

FINISHING TOUCHES

Global grook

If we want Peace,
    the things we must
accomplish
    to preserve it
are, first,
    to win each other's trust;
and, second,
    to deserve it.

HYGIENE

A grook with no reference
whatever to the two-party system

To wear a shirt
        that's relatively clean
you needn't ever
        launder off the dirt—
if you possess
        two shirts to choose between
and always change
        into the cleaner shirt.

PERFECTION

Perfection, when it reaches the degree
by certain panegyricists conceived,
is something far too wonderful to see:
it has to be described to be believed.

OUR OWN MOTES

The errors hardest
to condone
in other people
are one's own.

THE HELPING HAND

Good-neighbour grook

We perceive that we must
do our bit, on the score
of community labours;
so we each sweep the dust
from in front of our door
to in front of our neighbour's.

THE BOAST

It is the boast
        of modern man
to do at most
        the least he can.

TECHNICALLY SPEAKING

People with
    a bit of skill
are predestined
    to fare ill.

FEAR FRUITFULLY

Don't be scared
    by every panic-scare appearing;
don't believe
    in every transient reprieve;
but believe
    it will be better than you're fearing
when you fear
    it will be worse than you believe.

FRUSTRATED YOUNG MAN

Grook about a contemporary phenomenon

> No wonder the fellow
>   is fast turning mad
> with gloom and frustration
>   and doubt.
> It must be unbearable
>   being so sad
> with nothing to be it
>   about.

ON TAKING YOUR TIME

Time arrives all the time;
and the only true crime
is the way we defile it
    with worry.
For inadequate time
is that species of time
you encounter
    whenever you hurry.

ALL THE DIFFERENCE

Choosing would be
easy if a
diff'rence didn't
make things differ.

WHY DO THE CHIMPS LOOK WORRIED?

Anthropomorphological grook

When the Apes became Mankind
just a few were left behind.
    Some are still around.
Grey, neurotic, anxious, lined, —
can it be that they've divined
    whither they are bound?

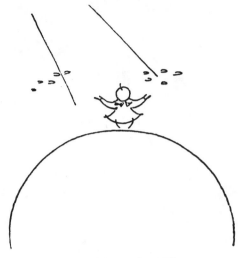

INTERVIEWEE

Am I pro, or anti, or ex, or ult-
    ra this, or that, or the other cult?
I am questioned with such pertinacity
    that, once for all, I can only say
    I am simply here on a passing stay
in a perfectly private capacity.

WEAKNESS THROUGH STRENGTH

Fanatics
may defend
        a point of view
so strongly
as to prove
        it can't be true.

UNQUALIFIED QUALIFICATION

To a friend,
in case he misunderstand me

I grant you, I attacked your foe;
but this, I feel you ought to know,
is something you should not construe
to mean that I agree with you.

CRANIAL CAPACITY

Portrait of a cerebral type

Back of that myopic face
every fact he's lived to trace
lies cross-indexed in its place
    with notes and variorum.
His collection grows apace,
and compels him to displace
every inch of working space
    to amplify the storeroom.

COLOQUINT

When old Coloquint
    is annoyed with me
he tells me as much
    with vim;
but that doesn't mean
    that I have to be,
for my part,
    annoyed with him.

But this is beyond
    his grasp—and so
he equally
    fails to see
that that's what annoys me,
    whether or no
the fellow's
    annoyed with me.

TELEPHONIC COMMUNICATIONS

Sparrows in the wintertime
    perch along the wires
cherishing the frozen songs
    they have no heart to sing,
fluffing out their feathers
    to conserve their inner fires,
waiting for the warmer airs
    that summertime will bring.

Troubadours a-wandering
    with summer-hearted lyres
recognize these scatterings
    of crotchets on a string:
wintertime notations
    of the melodies of Spring.

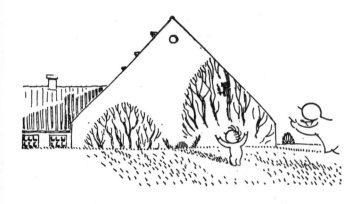

WILLOW PATTERN

The winter sun
gilds the bare willow trees; their shadows, tall
and starkly silhouetted, overrun
    my whitewashed wall.

The strength life owns
is such, that vivid life is what one sees
in the mere shadows of denuded bones
    of living trees.

A GROOK ABOUT A RED ROSE

I gave my love a rose of purest red.
All night it stood blushing beside her bed.
One petal fell; then two; and then a score:
It won't believe in budding any more.

ALREADY —

We now approach the season
when hope, in spite of reason,
   proclaims that Spring is on the way
      and Winter almost past;
when expectations flower
with every passing shower,
   and anxious hearts begin to say:
      already! and: at last!

BEECH GREEN

Colourgrook

The beech wood is more green this Spring
    than it has ever been.
One can't believe that anything
    could ever be so green.

Here is a green to ease the mind,
    and recreate the will;
but shut your eyes, and you will find
    its scent is greener still.

ADDRESS TO MY BELOVED

Some girls I worship from afar
    to passionate excess.
But when I meet them face to face
    I love them rather less.

Some other girls I love afresh
    each time I meet again.
It's not until they're out of sight
    that love begins to wane.

But you alone, my love, I love
    wherever you may be.
So you can stay, or go away,—
    it's all the same to me.

EXPERIENCE

A sigh

All we know
we learn to doubt
in life's successive schools.
Which goes to show
we started out
unutterable fools.

HABIT

A grook on prudery

The Truth that's naked
        and unadorned
affronts our culture
        as much as Babbitt's;
and now, as ever,
        the lady's scorned
unless she is dressed
        in conventional habits.

THE MIRROR

Mirrors have one limitation: You can't
    either by hook or by crook
use them to see how you look when you aren't
    looking to see how you look.

SPIRITUAL HEIRS

A grook addressed to Parnassus

O Master Minds of bygone ages,
you are our touchstones and our gauges:
we search our times and wonder who
could be a second—one of you.

But, Great Ones, is it worth pursuing
this fantasy of second-youing?
The me that seems to me worth being
has quite enough to do with meing.

ON AVOIDING EXCESS

Temperance grook

Yes, alcohol
    may be enjoyed
        in moderation
            with propriety;
but do for all
    the world avoid
        intoxication
            and sobriety.

CULTURE

A grook for vultures

Culture's the cultures
        of what's left behind
after a culture's
        departed.
Yet there's a problem
        that troubles my mind:
back in the innocent
        dawn of mankind,
how did it ever
        get started?

THE SOCIAL ROUND

Those smart invitations
    on smart people's shelves
that smart people send
    one another,
are summons to those
    who are bored by themselves
to come and be bored
    by each other.

WITHIN REACH

A grook on keeping order

Oh, it's grand when the things
   that you can't do without
have at last got so
   hopelessly strayed,
that regardless of where
   you start rooting about,
you will hit upon one
   you'd mislaid.

ENDOWMENT

However excellent
    intelligence,
yet there is one endowment
    to outgo it:
and that is
    to possess so little sense
you haven't even
    sense enough to know it.

39

ALMOST HUMAN

The thinking elevator,
so the makers proudly say,
will optimize its program
in an almost human way.
And truly, the resemblance
is uncomfortably strong:
it isn't merely thinking,
it's even thinking wrong.

GROWTH GROOK

Lying in the meadow grass
    I know that life is growing,
know that at this moment it's
    the only thing worth knowing.
Here my life flows onwards
    with Nature's living flow.
If it stopped its whispering
    the grass could hear me grow.

LIVING IN THE MOMENT

To live in the moment's a well-worn routine
        that most of the world has perfected;
for some, it's the moment that's already been,
        for others, — the one that's expected.

Yet no sort of magic can kindle anew
        a past that is over forever,
nor summon the future before it is due:
        our moment is now—or it's never.

So brief is the moment in which we may live,
        and future or past it isn't.
Whoever would know of what life has to give
        must gratefully welcome the present.

QUIET NIGHT

I'm feeling somewhat
       indisposed,
and so's my Muse,
       I've diagnosed.
So all exertion
       we'll avoid:
we'll put ourselves to bed
       with Freud.

LOOK ANEW

If you look anew
    with every new day's dawning,
as aware as though
    the world had just begun,
you will fill your life
    with meaning every morning,
but apart from that
    get very little done.

MUSA MEWS

My Muse—who swears she's mine forever,
    and means it, too—
made a remark I must endeavour
    to misconstrue.
She murmured: 'Don't you think we're clever?
    Compared to you?'

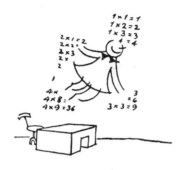

MULTIPLOY

What would I choose to be
if I were able?
I'd be the
multiplication table.
Natural laws
never enter its mind:
It simply applies
when it feels inclined.

TECHNIQUE

Recipe

The height of
    technical felicity
is to combine
    sublime simplicity
with just sufficient
    ingenuities
to show how difficult
    to do it is.

TWO HALF — TRUTHS

Half of a truth is often aired,
    and often proved correct:
it's sensible to be prepared
    for what you don't expect.

The other half is minimized,
    or totally neglected:
It's wiser still to be surprised
    by what you most expected.

THE PLAGIARIST

The plagiarist
    embodies
a naive
    miscalculation
he apes
    originality
by dint of
    imitation.

ASPIRATION

A tight-rope artiste, whose abilities
    made audiences gasp and perspire,
rejected her critics' civilities,
and aimed at still greater agilities.
    Her ultimate exploit was dire.
    For she vowed
    to the crowd
    that had come to admire:
    today I shall try it
    without any wire;
    for those who to difficult arts
    would aspire
must practise on impossibilities.

THE SHAPE OF TRUTH

A fable

A sage, who had filled his glass
    at the fountain of truth,
said, in a statement
    that later became canonical,
to his disciples,
    patterns of eager youth:
'I have seen truth itself;
    and it is conical'.

EVENING AND MORNING SONG

About falling asleep and waking up

The world disappears,
a loop running smaller, until
the thread is drawn out,
and the space it encloses is nil.

Newborn of nothing,
reluctantly starting to be,
fumbling awareness awakens
and finds that it's me.

ADMONITION TO RECITERS

Pedagogic grook

Let spoken poetry stand alone,
    as printed on the air.
Let no sweet soulfulness of tone
    be manifested there.

Whatever soul the words embrace
    the words alone must state:
the moment they are put in place
    sweet-souling comes too late.

TITLE INDEX

ADDRESS TO MY BELOVED 30
ADMONITION TO RECITERS 53
A GROOK ABOUT A RED ROSE 27
ALL THE DIFFERENCE 18
ALMOST HUMAN 40
ALREADY 28
ASPIRATION 50
BEECH GREEN 29
COLOQUINT.................................. 24
CRANIAL CAPACITY 23
CULTURE 36
DATES 5
ENDOWMENT 39
EVENING AND MORNING SONG 52
EXPERIENCE 31
FEAR FRUITFULLY............................ 15
FINISHING TOUCHES......................... 8
FRUSTRATED YOUNG MAN 16
GROWTH GROOK 41
HABIT 32
HYGIENE 9
INTERVIEWEE 20
LIVING IN THE MOMENT 42
LOOK ANEW 44
MULTIPLOY.................................. 46
MUSA MEWS 45
ON AVOIDING EXCESS 35
ON TAKING YOUR TIME 17
OUR OWN MOTES 11
PERFECTION................................. 10
POPULAR RENOWN.......................... 3
QUIET NIGHT 43
ROAD HOGS................................. 4
SPIRITUAL HEIRS 34
TECHNICALLY SPEAKING...................... 14

TECHNIQUE 47
TELEPHONIC COMMUNICATIONS 25
THE BOAST 13
THE COMMON WELL 6
THE GREAT AND THE SMALL 1
THE HELPING HAND 12
THE MIRROR...................................... 33
THE PLAGIARIST 49
THE RECALCITRANT MEDIUM 2
THE SHAPE OF TRUTH 51
THE SOCIAL ROUND 37
TWO HALF — TRUTHS 48
UNQUALIFIED QUALIFICATION 22
UP TO THE MINUTE 7
WEAKNESS THROUGH STRENGTH 21
WHY DO THE CHIMPS LOOK WORRIED? 19
WILLOW PATTERN 26
WITHIN REACH 38

First line index

A box of dates 5
All we know 31
Am I pro, or anti, or ex, or ult- 20
A Sage, who had filled his glass 51
A tight-rope artiste, whose abilities 50
Back of that myopic face 23
Choosing would be 18
Culture's the cultures 36
Don't be scared 15
Does no one read the Highway Code? 4
Fanatics 21
Half of a truth is often aired 48
However excellent 39
If we want Peace 8
If you look anew 44
I gave my love a rose of purest red 27
I grant you, I attacked your foe 22
I'm feeling somewhat 43
It is the boast 13
Let spoken poetry stand alone 53
Lying in the meadow grass 41
Mirrors have one limitation: You can't 33
My Muse—who swears she's mine forever 45
No wonder the fellow 16
Oh, it's grand when the things 38
O Master Minds of bygone ages 34
Perfection, when it reaches the degree 10
People with 14
Some girls I worship from afar 30
Sparrows in the wintertime 25
Strive after popular renown 3
The beech wood is more green this Spring 29
The errors hardest 11
The height of 47
The plagiarist 49
The thinking elevator 40

The Truth that's naked 32
The unyielding medium's 2
The well you invite us to drink of 6
The winter sun 26
The world disappears 52
Those smart invitations......................... 37
Time arrives all the time........................ 17
To live in the moment's a well-worn routine 42
To wear a shirt 9
We now approach the season 28
We think of our age 7
We perceive that we must 12
What would I choose to be....................... 46
When great things 1
When old Coloquint 24
When the Apes became Mankind 19
Yes, alcohol 35